The Bakerloo Line

A SHORT HISTORY

by

M. A. C. Horne

1990
Published by Douglas Rose
35 Summers Lane, North Finchley, London N12 0PE
but
Distributed by Nebulous Books
Raven Square, Alton, Hampshire GU34 2LL

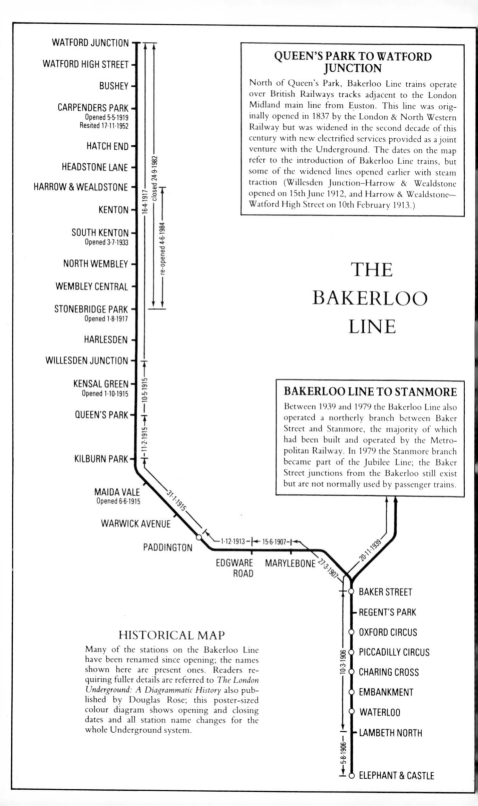

WATFORD JUNCTION
WATFORD HIGH STREET
BUSHEY
CARPENDERS PARK
Opened 5·5·1919
Resited 17·11·1952
HATCH END
HEADSTONE LANE
HARROW & WEALDSTONE
KENTON
SOUTH KENTON
Opened 3·7·1933
NORTH WEMBLEY
WEMBLEY CENTRAL
STONEBRIDGE PARK
Opened 1·8·1917
HARLESDEN
WILLESDEN JUNCTION
KENSAL GREEN
Opened 1·10·1915
QUEEN'S PARK
KILBURN PARK
MAIDA VALE
Opened 6·6·1915
WARWICK AVENUE
PADDINGTON
EDGWARE ROAD
MARYLEBONE

16·4·1917
closed 24·9·1982
re-opened 4·6·1984
10·5·1915
11·2·1915
31·1·1915
1·12·1913
15·6·1907
27·3·1907
20·11·1939

BAKER STREET
REGENT'S PARK
OXFORD CIRCUS
PICCADILLY CIRCUS
CHARING CROSS
EMBANKMENT
WATERLOO
LAMBETH NORTH
ELEPHANT & CASTLE

10·3·1906
5·8·1906

QUEEN'S PARK TO WATFORD JUNCTION

North of Queen's Park, Bakerloo Line trains operate over British Railways tracks adjacent to the London Midland main line from Euston. This line was originally opened in 1837 by the London & North Western Railway but was widened in the second decade of this century with new electrified services provided as a joint venture with the Underground. The dates on the map refer to the introduction of Bakerloo Line trains, but some of the widened lines opened earlier with steam traction (Willesden Junction–Harrow & Wealdstone opened on 15th June 1912, and Harrow & Wealdstone— Watford High Street on 10th February 1913.)

THE BAKERLOO LINE

BAKERLOO LINE TO STANMORE

Between 1939 and 1979 the Bakerloo Line also operated a northerly branch between Baker Street and Stanmore, the majority of which had been built and operated by the Metropolitan Railway. In 1979 the Stanmore branch became part of the Jubilee Line; the Baker Street junctions from the Bakerloo still exist but are not normally used by passenger trains.

HISTORICAL MAP

Many of the stations on the Bakerloo Line have been renamed since opening; the names shown here are present ones. Readers requiring fuller details are referred to *The London Underground: A Diagrammatic History* also published by Douglas Rose; this poster-sized colour diagram shows opening and closing dates and all station name changes for the whole Underground system.

The Strand entrance to Trafalgar Square station (now called Charing Cross) shortly after the Bakerloo Line opened. Although not easily visible in this photograph, the right-hand end of the curved sign gives running times from this station and includes that for Paddington, which is covered by a paper slip as it was not constructed for some years more. The season tickets referred to in the main sign were issued between November 1906 and September 1908.

*London Transport Museum**

To C. E. L.

The Bakerloo Line: A Short History
by M. A. C. Horne
ISBN 1 870354 03 6
First published in June 1990
© Copyright M. A. C. Horne

Other short histories in this series by M. A. C. Horne
 THE NORTHERN LINE
 THE CENTRAL LINE
 THE VICTORIA LINE

The author and publisher wish to acknowledge the assistance of
Peter Bancroft, Paul Hadley, Suzanne Tagg, and
particularly to Jonathan Roberts and John Liffen.

Photographs marked with an asterisk (*) are reproduced
by kind permission of the London Transport Museum. Copy
prints may be ordered from the Museum's Photo Library.

The text in this book has been set in
Lintotype Garamond No.3 10/11pt and 8/8½pt,
with appropriate italic and small caps,
on a Linotron 300.

Typeset by Trintype Limited, Wellingborough NN8 2QR
Cover design by Art Attack, London SW9 6AR,
from an idea by M. A. C. Horne.
Printed by Printline (Offset) Limited, London N7 8EJ

THE BAKERLOO LINE is a product of the turn-of-the-century boom in tube railway construction, and is over eighty years old. The 6·7 miles (10·7km) from Elephant & Castle to Queen's Park is nearly all within the Underground's familiar deep-level tube environment, but the line is unusual in that the remaining 7·7 miles (12·3km) to Harrow & Wealdstone is shared with British Rail's Watford local service, and itself used to serve Watford. For nearly half its present life the Bakerloo Line also served the Middlesex suburbs of Willesden Green, Wembley Park and Stanmore by means of a branch line diverging at Baker Street. However, the Stanmore branch was transferred a decade ago to the then new Jubilee Line, and its tube history will be covered in detail in the Jubilee Line book.

The desire for an underground link between the north side of the river and the London terminus of the London & South Western Railway (LSWR) at Waterloo was beset with difficulty for nearly forty years. An early scheme was the Waterloo & Whitehall Railway, which dated back to 1865. This was intended to run between Great Scotland Yard (near Charing Cross) and Waterloo (LSWR) station, and was interesting in that it reflected an early desire to put a city-centre railway beneath street and river in relatively small sized tunnels and wrought iron tubes.

Electric traction had not even reached the advanced stage of infancy and to propel the trains pneumatic power was proposed, avoiding the need for steam locomotives. This system followed promising results obtained from experimental work for a mail-conveying pneumatic railway built between Euston and Holborn (opened in 1865). Here the carriages were fitted with a flexible flange which prevented air from passing the carriage in the tunnel. A difference between the air pressures in the tunnel either side of the carriage would therefore cause it to move. The system was a technical success, if not a commercial one.

A considerable amount of construction was undertaken on the Waterloo & Whitehall scheme, but an untimely financial crisis in 1866 made it impossible to raise the additional capital needed to complete the work. With cash lacking the company could not survive and its fate was sealed, although its formal demise was not until 1882. The opening of the South Eastern Railway's station at Waterloo in 1869 (linking the area with Charing Cross) also diminished the need for another cross-river railway on a similar route.

A later proposal was known as the Charing Cross & Waterloo Electric Railway, which obtained an Act of Incorporation in August 1882. This was a cut-and-cover scheme although the line beneath the river was to be carried in twin iron caissons lowered into a trench – similar to the Waterloo & Whitehall proposal. The northern terminus was to be near Trafalgar Square, while the southern terminus was beneath the LSWR's Waterloo station, some five-eighths of a mile away. The enabling Act provided for first, second and third class passengers (at maximum fares of sixpence, fourpence and threepence respectively). With Dr. C.W. Siemens as its electrical engineer this might well have emerged as the first electric underground railway in London, but adequate finance was not forthcoming and almost no construction work was undertaken, the company becoming defunct by a further Act of 1885. Siemens's death in 1883 must have been a severe blow to the company's future.

The Baker Street & Waterloo Railway (BS&WR) was a more ambitious scheme yet. The first evidence of moves to provide a railway between these two points emerged in 1891 when an attempt was made to promote a Bill in Parliament. In addition to the Charing Cross–Waterloo link, which formed the southern end of the proposal, it was to continue northwards to upper Baker Street. This alignment would considerably improve north–south communication across central London, and this factor was reflected in the first prospective name of the concern – the North & South London Railway. The 3-mile line was to have been constructed in twin iron-lined tube tunnels, the success of this system having been proved by the City & South London Railway which had opened in 1890 as the first electric tube railway in the world.

Under its revised name, the BS&WR was eventually incorporated by an Act of Parliament of 28th March 1893. The extremities of the route were described as New Street (now Melcombe Street) near Upper Baker Street, to the southern side of James Street, near Lower Marsh. In common with certain other early tube schemes the carriage of both first and second class passengers was allowed for, at maximum rates of twopence or threepence a mile respectively. The carriage of mails and small parcels was catered for, but goods traffic was prohibited. A number of 'parliamentary' trains, calling at all stations, was required at the usual penny a mile rate. Raising the finance again proved to be a major obstacle and the company lay virtually dormant for some years.

In 1896 the BS&WR remained optimistic about overcoming its financial difficulties and obtained a second Act of Parliament; this authorized an extension of time, a further increase in capital, and an almost quarter-mile projection beneath New Street and Melcombe Place to the Marylebone station of the Great Central Railway, then under construction. This new station was not otherwise conveniently served by existing underground railways. Although two of the BS&WR's board were also directors of the LSWR the latter company were disinclined to offer financial assistance to the tube company, evidently believing that the feeder traffic did not warrant the (considerable) outlay.

In the event help came from the direction of a mining finance company, just as it had done (in 1895) on the Central London Railway. This time it was the London & Globe Finance Corporation which offered its help, and a suitable contract was signed between the two concerns on 4th November 1897. In due course the BS&WR Board was replaced by one identical to that of the London & Globe.

But this company was one a number of which one Whitaker Wright was in sole effective control. Wright, though an Englishman, had made his fortune in the United States in mine prospecting, and on his return to his native country lived in mildly eccentric affluence. He set up business in the City, and gradually spawned a network of finance companies, many of which were involved in mining finance. His companies were characterised by the existence on their Boards of various dignitaries of whom few, if any, took part in the running of the companies. The London & Globe became the main contractors for the new railway and took upon themselves the responsibility for bringing the new line into being.

The construction of the tunnels was subcontracted to Perry & Company. Work began in August 1898 from a staging on the River Thames near Hungerford Bridge, from which point two shafts were sunk. The river staging avoided the need to find suitable land sites in central London while allowing for removal of spoil and delivery of materials by barge. Amongst other facilities provided on the staging were numerous workshops and a small power station for temporary power and lighting in the tunnels. The twin running tunnels, of 11ft 8¼ins (3.56m) diameter, were to be driven in both directions from the bottom of these shafts, together with additional shafts along the line of route. All tunnels were to be driven by hydraulically powered 'Greathead' tunnelling shields, successfully used on the City & South London. Stations were to be situated at: Waterloo (beneath the LSWR), Charing Cross (beneath the District Railway station), Trafalgar Square, Piccadilly Circus, Oxford Circus, Baker Street and Marylebone.

Another extension of time was granted by a third Act of Parliament, in August 1899, by which time the company had expended some £300,000. This Act also authorized the southern end of the line to deviate slightly westwards to terminate at the south east end of Addington Street, allowing for an improved depot and power station arrangement (the original site having been in Lower Marsh). Also authorized were subways from the ticket hall area at Trafalgar Square station leading to various nearby street corners.

In 1900 the BS&WR obtained a fourth Act of Parliament which authorized two further extensions. At the north end a route was sanctioned from Marylebone to Paddington (Great Western Railway) station (near the junction of Bishops Road and Gloucester Terrace); an

The construction of the Bakerloo began from this staging in the river just upstream of Hungerford Bridge. Here two shafts were sunk, materials delivered and spoil removed. Curiously, another more familiar view of the staging has often been reproduced back-to-front, giving the impression that the staging was downstream of the bridge. *Bakerloo opening brochure*

intermediate station was visualized at Edgware Road, apparently on the west side of that road. It had also been the intention to build a branch line from a point north of Oxford Circus to Euston, but this was not authorized in the 1900 Act and was not pursued.

At the southern end of the line the company was also authorized to project beyond Waterloo to the busy Elephant & Castle (with subway connection to the nearby City & South London Railway station) – this nearly mile-long extension terminated in the New Kent Road. The company was to construct the Elephant & Castle ticket hall beneath the busy road junction itself, with subway entrances from various street corners. In addition to these the 1900 Act authorized a revised depot and power station site near St. George's Circus, Southwark, and the construction of a 650-yard link from the depot to the main BS&WR route. When work began, the subcontract for the northern extension went to Perry & Company, while that for the depot and Elephant & Castle extension went to John Mowlem.

But the London & Globe was not all it appeared to be, and when some of Wright's ventures sustained heavy losses a number of financial irregularities were exposed which showed several 'successful' companies to be in severe trouble. At the close of 1900 the London &

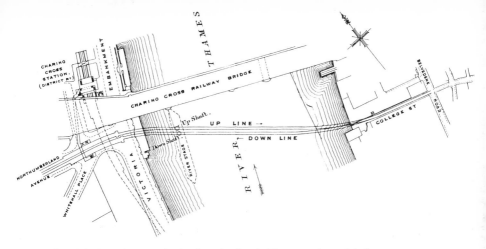

Diagram of the Bakerloo as it runs under the river, showing the Thames staging and shafts.

Institution of Civil Engineers, 1902

Globe and some associated companies announced their insolvency, the crash dragging down in its wake numerous firms of stockbrokers. Wright maintained his composure until the end of 1901 when he was subjected to a public examination. His exposure as a potential fraud encouraged him to withdraw to Paris.

The majesty of the law was rather slow in pursuing justice but was hastened by angry creditors who short-circuited the inaction of the Attorney General. As soon as the intention to prosecute was known Wright attempted to flee to the United States – he was arrested on arrival and eventually extradited back to London where he was successfully prosecuted for publishing false balance sheets and accounts. The case would have been heard at the Old Bailey but for an application by Wright's Counsel to have it heard at the Royal Courts of Justice under Civil, rather than Criminal procedures. This rearrangement allowed Wright his final opportunity to cheat his fellows. Had he been convicted at the Bailey then Police procedures would have been followed and immediate imprisonment was ensured. At the Law Courts matters were dealt with rather differently and Wright was allowed to consult his advisors unsupervised in a private room. He eluded his seven-year prison sentence by means of a cyanide capsule, and it was with considerable embarrassment that upon his body was found not only a second capsule but a revolver, which he had presumably had in court with him. Upon such people did the future London Underground depend!

Against this colourful and intriguing background the BS&WR had been partially built, representing some of the more solid assets of the London & Globe. Substantial progress had been made on the running tunnels and on a few of the station tunnels, and some work on the

9

depot site had been started. But the collapse of the financial backing caused work to be drastically scaled down, and throughout 1901 much of the railway workings became virtually moribund. A little money trickled in from share calls from non-institutional shareholders, and on a monthly basis the BS&WR paid the sub-contractors directly for the small amount of work pushed ahead, mainly between the river and Oxford Circus.

By August 1901 the state of affairs was as follows. The southbound tunnel was complete from the river shaft to a point 90 yards southwards (this required working in compressed air). North of the river shaft the same tunnel had just been completed from the river to Regent Street, just north of Conduit Street. The station tunnels had been bored at Embankment, Trafalgar Square and Piccadilly Circus. The northbound tunnel was complete from Waterloo station tunnel (of which 20 yards had been excavated) to a point in Regent Street 107 yards north of Vigo Street, where work had been suspended on 4th May 1901. The station tunnels had been excavated at Trafalgar Square. and Piccadilly Circus, but at Embankment a small-bore tunnel had been driven through the station site, and the tunnel required enlarging. From the same date work had been suspended on the tunnel drives southwards from Baker Street, the southbound tunnel having reached a point near Park Square, and the northbound tunnel extending to Portland Place, just south of Park Crescent. It would appear that one station tunnel was complete at Baker Street while the other required opening out from temporary running tunnel, built to expedite progress.

While the construction of the railway had been progressing, there were others who had been taking an interest in London's public transport affairs. Prior to the Globe's collapse at the end of 1900 negotiations had already been taking place with an American syndicate headed by Albert L. Johnson with a view to its taking over the Baker Street & Waterloo interests; presumably the ailing Globe would have been grateful to exchange its long-term interests in the railway for hard cash. The negotiations were never completed, apparently being pre-empted by events. (Johnson was involved in the American tramroad industry and appears to have come to London in 1899 to promote an electric railway from London to Brighton. He died in Brooklyn in July 1901).

It was another American who came to the railway's rescue after the Globe had sunk. This time the man was Charles Tyson Yerkes, who had made his particular fortune in Philadelphia and Chicago by building and improving city transport, especially by modernizing and electrifying existing old-fashioned systems. He did this with no lack of criticism, especially of his motives. His forte was to carry out property speculation in areas likely to benefit from improved transport services. He had been introduced to similar problems and opportunities in London and had taken an interest in them. By 1900 his syndicate had acquired the steam-hauled Metropolitan District Railway (MDR) and several tube railway schemes. The former he intended to electrify and completely re-equip, and the latter he intended to construct from new. Agreement between the Baker Street & Waterloo, the Globe's liquidators and Yerkes's Metropolitan District Electric Traction Company was reached in March 1902, and the future of the tube scheme was secured.

Later during the same year the Yerkes syndicate formed a much larger and more flexible holding company known as the Underground Electric Railways Company of London Limited (UERL), and this took overall control of his various tube schemes as well as the MDR and the Traction company. The UERL was to run much of London's transport for the next thirty-one years.

In addition to the BS&WR, two other tubes emerged under the Yerkes banner, though Yerkes's death in 1905 meant he never saw them in operation. The other two companies were the Great Northern, Piccadilly & Brompton Railway (GNP&BR) and the Charing Cross, Euston & Hampstead Railway (CCE&HR). These cumbersome titles were soon shortened to Piccadilly Tube and Hampstead Tube in the eyes of the public, and were later to form trunk sections of what are now (respectively) the Piccadilly and Northern Lines.

The UERL was appointed the main contractor for all three Yerkes tube railways and so far as possible similar standards and styles were adopted. The BS&WR differed from its two compatriots in that a substantial amount had already been built and it was extremely difficult to adapt some of this work to suit the new standard. Thus BS&WR platforms were shorter than on the other two lines, and the layouts of the partly constructed stations were somewhat awkward. Indeed the layout at Oxford Circus was so objectionable that the company desired to make some alterations. By this time the Board of Trade (responsible for approving the designs) had itself set higher standards of access and safety for new construction and took the opportunity to protest at the arrangements at Oxford Circus. This resulted in major reconstruction of the low-level passages, and gives Oxford Circus the unusual privilege of being the only tube station to be substantially rebuilt before it even opened.

The BS&WR's fifth Act (of 1902) further extended the authorized time for completing the railway, and noted in the preamble that so far £944,702 had been expended and the railway was largely complete from Waterloo to Oxford Circus. In 1903 another Act authorized the taking of additional lands near Lambeth Christ Church, and also authorized the company to make agreement with the UERL for

The original Bakerloo Line cars were brought down from Manchester by train and then conveyed by road from Camden goods depot to London Road depot. Although mechanical haulage was tried the majority of the fleet was moved, a car at a time, by horse power.
'Railway Magazine' March 1906

the supply of electricity to the BS&WR (avoiding the need for the BS&WR to build its own power station at the St George's Circus depot, better known as London Road depot). A second Act of 1903 further extended the railway's time to complete the works.

By March 1903 some 80 per cent of the running tunnels were complete from Waterloo to Dorset Square and all authorized station tunnels were complete on that section other than one at Waterloo. Little work had been undertaken south of Waterloo but contractors had just begun operations on the future depot site. A year later the running tunnels north of Waterloo were complete, except for the crossover north of Baker Street; work was also in progress on equipping some of the station sites. South of Waterloo about a quarter of the depot excavation had been completed and the running tunnels were making good progress.

In 1904 yet another Act authorized construction of two additional stations, at Kennington Road (now Lambeth North) and Regent's Park. The tunnelling was well advanced and this necessitated the new station tunnels being constructed from around the existing running tunnels. The Act also provided powers to construct a station at Edgware Road, on the eastern side of that road, on the corner of Bell Street (superseding the earlier proposal for a station on the other side of the road). At this station the running tunnels were not yet started and the station could be built conventionally.

By July 1904 platforms were being installed at several stations and most of the low-level subway works were nearly complete. South of Waterloo good progress was being made with tunnelling and with excavation of the depot site. Work on the Edgware Road extension had also begun.

Early in 1905 the tunnels were complete from Elephant & Castle to Baker Street except for a short stretch at Elephant & Castle; about half the track had also been laid. Some of the station superstructures had been started, platform installation continued with some tiling work now under way. About a third of the depot site remained unexcavated but work on erecting some of the buildings had begun. The electrical work had started, as had preparation for the lifts. The rolling stock was also on order.

Towards the end of 1905 the line had largely taken shape and much of the rolling stock had already been delivered to the depot. Although locomotive haulage had been contemplated at first, the success of multiple-unit operation on the Central London Railway showed the clear superiority of that system and the BS&WR followed suit. The 108 cars were built in the USA by the American Car & Foundry Company and shipped in a dismantled state to Trafford Park in Manchester. Here they were assembled and marshalled into trains which were then conveyed by rail to Camden goods depot. Individual cars were then hauled by road each night (generally using horses) to London Road depot, where they carefully negotiated the sharp turn and steep gradient into the yard. The first car arrived on 12th September 1905.

London Road depot was the main stabling facility and the only works on the Bakerloo. The site was very cramped and below ground level; on the left is the ramp down which the new cars were delivered, with the car hoist at its end. The connection with the main line was via a single track tunnel just north of Kennington Road station (now Lambeth North). A separate shunting tunnel was also provided. The depot lost its main repair facilities when Neasden depot became available, but it remains a stabling point. *Bakerloo opening brochure*

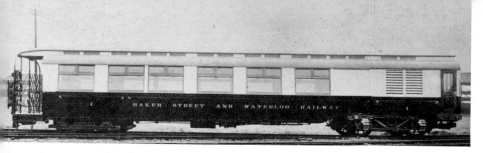

One of the motor cars used when the line opened. Passengers entered the car from the gated end (left) through the end door. The driving cab (right) was next to the motor bogie, which the underframe was carried over to clear. An equipment compartment (and four passenger seats) was mounted over the bogie. Trailer cars had a gate entrance at both ends of the car.

*London Transport Museum**

The cars were divided into three types, there being 36 of each. The motor cars had a driving cab at one end and at the other was a gated entrance platform allowing access to the car interior through end doors. Trailer cars had no motors or equipment compartments and had gated platforms at both ends; control trailers were similar but had drivers' control equipment mounted on one of the gated platforms. The car exteriors were finished in a maroon and cream livery.

In order for electricity to be taken from the UERL's central generating station at Lots Road (near Chelsea Creek) it was necessary for high tension feeder cables to be brought to a substation and distribution point at Charing Cross (above the BS&WR's station), from which point power was distributed to the line's other substations at London Road and Baker Street. Current was supplied to the trains via two conductor rails (one between the running rails and the other outside) at around 600 volts d.c.

Signalling was substantially automatic, using a system already tried in America and designed by Westinghouse (a similar system was successfully used on the Metropolitan District Railway from 1905). This used electrically energised track circuits which operated pneumatically controlled signals, where spectacle plates moved to show the appropriate coloured light. At each stop signal a pneumatically controlled lever next to the running rails, called a 'trainstop', was raised when a red aspect was shown; this was designed to engage with a 'tripcock' on a passing train and thus apply the emergency brakes. The lever lay flat when a green signal was shown. This type of safety device is still in use today. At stations where crossovers existed the signals were semi-automatic and were under the overriding control of a signalman. Both signals and points were fully interlocked and controlled from a miniature lever frame, the signalman establishing the position of trains from an illuminated track diagram.

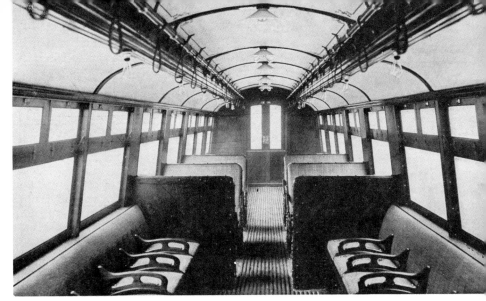

Interior of one of the original Bakerloo cars.   *Bakerloo opening brochure*

Where full station buildings were provided they were of a standard general design used throughout the three UERL tubes but adapted to the requirements of individual sites. Designed by Leslie W. Green each station was a two-storey structure clothed in ruby red glazed terracotta. At Regent's Park and Trafalgar Square stations the sites required ticket halls below ground level and access from the street was via steps and subways, an extensive system in the case of Trafalgar Square. At Charing Cross, which the BS&WR called Embankment, access to the tube railway was gained by means of a long inclined subway leading down from the existing MDR Charing Cross station, and no separate station building was constructed. Over the river, at Waterloo, much work had already been completed before Leslie Green's designs emerged, and the ticket hall reflected earlier plans, though finishings to an entrance in York Road did reflect Green's style.

At platform level the decor originally planned appears to have followed the practice of the City & South and Central London Railways, with glazed white tiling covering the entire platform tunnel vault, maximising the reflection of precious lighting. Tiling work on this theme was started by early 1904 at Trafalgar Square. But while this was going on Yerkes took an interest in the platform finishings, which appears to have resulted in experimental finishes at another station, probably Waterloo. The result was a patterned tiling scheme devised for each station. These are generally attributed to Leslie Green and on the whole were favourably reviewed in the press.

15

The Evening News.

ONE HALFPENNY.

LONDON : WEDNESDAY, MARCH 7, 1906.

NO. 7,608.

500,000 SQUARE MILES OF SUNSHINE.	THE BAKER-LOO.	THE HIRE-PURCHASE SEIZURE.	1,000 GUESTS	M.P. & HIS BROTHE'

500,000 SQUARE MILES OF SUNSHINE.

LONDON'S FORETASTE OF COMING SUMMER.

YEAR'S RECORD PASSED.

67 DEGREES IN THE SHADE THIS AFTERNOON.

...ing this afternoon tho shade re-
... as degrees —

THE BAKER-LOO.

Trial Trip of Baker-street and Waterloo Railway.

FIRST STRAPHANGER.

London's latest "Tuppenny Tube"—the Baker-street and Waterloo Railway—to-day carried its first passengers, and on Saturday will be open to the public.

The new line forms an important link in the elaborate system of "tube" electric railways, which, when all are completed, will give London the most modern and complete scheme of underground inter-communication in the world.

To-day an "Evening News" representative was permitted to travel on the new railway, now nearing completion after eight years' work.

The Baker-street and Waterloo Railway has already many memories for railway-men and financiers, for it was the last work of the late Mr. Yerkes, the Tube... and Whitaker Wright, the fallen...

THE HIRE-PURCHASE SEIZURE.

Miss Jewell in Tears Under Cross-examination.

1,000 GUESTS

Are Expected at To-night's Drawing Room in Dublin.

Our correspondent writes to-day :— full swing, and

M.P. & HIS BROTHE'

To-day's Hearing of the : Against Sir Alfred Thor

JUDGE'S SLIP OF PAP.

resumed to-day o

The birth of the name Bakerloo Line, Wednesday 7th March 1906, heading an article describing that day's press preview of the line. Whilst not universally applauded, the name quickly became popular.
'Evening News' 1906

The central portion of the new tube was ready for opening early in 1906, and for several weeks previously a full service was operated (without the benefit of passengers) to train and acclimatize the staff. The big day was Saturday 10th March. The opening ceremony was performed by the Chairman of the London County Council, Sir Edwin Cornwall MP, after which the line was heavily patronised for the remainder of the day. At this stage a service operated between Baker Street and Kennington Road.

Even though the company name was the Baker Street & Waterloo Railway, the tendency for colloquial names to be used in everyday parlance took an interesting turn at about the time of the railway's opening. The Evening News referred to the tube as the "Baker-loo" in one of its headlines; the name had a certain ring to it and in spite of adverse comment elsewhere the company itself started to use the name. Fortunately suggestions from some other papers (The Star referred to the line as "the 'Loo") were ignored. A little later the epithet 'tube' was officially suppressed in favour of 'Underground' or 'Railway', as appropriate. But 'Bakerloo' stuck, and is, of course, the name still with us today. The exact inventor of 'Bakerloo' is not easily discernible, but an obituary in the News Chronicle for 27th May 1933 attributes it to Captain G.H.F. Nichols who began his Fleet Street career as a reporter on the Evening News (though, intriguingly, not until a year after the line had opened).

However promising the interest in the line might have been on the opening day, traffic during the following few weeks was extremely disappointing and was a matter of some initial concern. It did not bode well for the other two lines which had not yet opened, and train lengths were substantially reduced. Fortunately matters improved after a few months and the railway soon established itself as the vital link its promoters envisaged. A factor in this may have been the abandonment in July 1906 of charging a flat fare of twopence in

The platforms at Oxford Circus were typical of most on the original section of the Bakerloo. Characterized by barrel-like tiled rings and decorative coloured panels, the stations were thematically similar though differing individually in colour and pattern. Main lighting was by electric arc lamps with incandescent bulbs provided for emergency use.

'The Car' 7th March 1906

favour of a charge relating to distance – fares varied between a penny and threepence in halfpenny steps.

Plans for what to do next at the northern end of the line were not settled, and went through several major revisions – and delays. It was clear that Paddington main line terminus, just half a mile from the Bakerloo's Edgware Road station, was an important location to serve. The BS&WR station at Paddington had been intended to be near Bishops Bridge Road, and connect with the Great Western station by means of a long subway beneath Eastbourne Terrace. This alignment appears to have been inherited from an abortive scheme of 1899 to extend the railway from Baker Street to Royal Oak, and thence to Willesden on the London & North Western Railway.

In the event it was decided not to seek powers for the portion west of Paddington in what became the company's 1900 Act. The proposed interchange there was not ideal and with the financial crisis and new ownership a start on the extension, at least westwards of Edgware Road, was discouraged. But Paddington remained the obvious traffic objective and a modified route was sought and obtained in the railway's 1906 Act which was shorter, deviating from the authorized route just west of Edgware Road station.

Whilst this brought the tube nearer to the main line station, and provided for a good interchange with the existing railways, the BS&WR would have terminated under the corner of Devonport Street and Grand Junction Road pointing due south-east. The disadvantage was the awkwardness of future extension in the direction most ripe for it, north-westwards into rural Middlesex. No work was carried out on the Bakerloo's 1906 Paddington scheme.

The remainder of the line opened piecemeal, being extended southwards to Elephant & Castle on 5th August 1906, and north-wards to Marylebone on 27th March 1907 and Edgware Road on 15th June 1907. The station at Marylebone was actually opened under the name Great Central, evidently reflecting the name of the company serving Marylebone main line station, with which there was subway access beneath Harewood Avenue. This, slightly odd, name continued until 15th April 1917 when the present name of Marylebone was adopted. Kennington Road station was renamed Westminster Bridge Road station on the same day as the railway's extension to Elephant & Castle. Both Edgware Road and Elephant & Castle stations had street level surface buildings in the Leslie Green style, the railway being prevented from building the sub-surface ticket hall at the latter station by restrictive clauses in the company's 1904 Act (put in at the insistence of the Southwark Borough Council). Great Central station had a single-storey station building, but the ticket hall and lift entrances were at basement level.

Although the initial passenger service terminated at Baker Street the trains nevertheless ran beyond, to the unopened Great Central station, where they reversed in the northbound tunnel. To allow this to be done a temporary signal cabin was built in the crossover tunnel just to the east of the station. A permanent signal cabin on the south-bound platform replaced the temporary one on Sunday 12th May 1907, from which date trains were extended to Edgware Road, and Great Central southbound platform came into use. Trains ran empty between Great Central and Edgware Road until the latter station was completed in June. A further signal box was introduced at Edgware Road when the railway arrived, and boxes then existed at Edgware Road, Great Central, Westminster Bridge Road, Elephant & Castle and at the depot outlet at London Road (this signal cabin was closed in 1915 and control of movements to or from the depot transferred to Westminster Bridge Road cabin). In addition to the main depot, sta-bling facilities existed for trains in siding tunnels beyond the plat-forms at both Edgware Road and Elephant & Castle.

The Bakerloo's compatriot lines, the Piccadilly and Hampstead tubes, opened respectively in December 1906 and June 1907, and all three provided a broadly similar style of service. The Bakerloo inter-connected with the Piccadilly at Piccadilly Circus, and shared a

Elephant & Castle station, photographed by the Bedford Lemere studio on 8th August 1907, typifies the Leslie Green style surface buildings on the Bakerloo railway. Above first floor level space was available for commercial use. *Royal Commission on the Historical Monuments of England*

common station building although separate lifts were provided. Through bookings existed between Bakerloo and the Piccadilly from the latter's opening and through fares between all the UERL tubes and the District Railway soon emerged. The system of through booking was soon extended to the other independent tube lines and some other railways. Physical interchange facilities already existed with the Central London Railway at Oxford Circus, the City & South London Railway at Elephant & Castle and the Metropolitan Railway at Baker Street. The first two of these had low-level interchange passages with interchange ticket offices in the subways – these closed when through bookings were introduced. In addition to through fares the three tubes soon adopted a common rule book, and company passes, staff working conditions and rolling stock all became interchangeable.

From 1909 agreement was reached between the UERL companies and the independent Central London, City & South London, Great Northern & City and Metropolitan Railways for the joint use of the word UNDERGROUND with large initial and final letters, and a narrow bar above and below each of the other letters. This was applied to station entrances to promote a common image, and at about the same time a joint map was produced for use on the respective companies' publicity.

The interdependence of the three UERL tubes was officially acknowledged in 1910 when the GNP&BR was renamed the London Electric Railway (LER) and absorbed the BS&W and CCE&H Railways. Thus the BS&WR (or Bakerloo Railway) now became the London Electric Railway's Bakerloo Line, and Bakerloo Line it has been ever since. This move allowed further economies to be made and a better pooling of resources amongst the three lines. Matters were taken a stage further in 1913 when the UERL took financial control of the City & South London and Central London Railways (also tubes). These companies retained their separate legal identities, but in 1915 a new pooling scheme was adopted between all the UERL lines which henceforth became operated as a single system. By then the London General Omnibus Company and various tramway companies were also part of the UERL fold.

A short-lived proposal for Bakerloo expansion emerged in 1908 when a junction was proposed at Edgware Road with another proposed tube line, the North West London Railway (originally authorized in 1899 to build a line from Marble Arch to Kilburn). The intention was for the Bakerloo to work the line north of Edgware Road, the Marble Arch portion being abandoned. As part of the proposal it was also intended to construct the Paddington extension, which would effectively operate as a Paddington–Edgware Road shuttle. From the Bakerloo's viewpoint the move captured the Paddington traffic whilst retaining the possibility of a future northerly extension, beyond Kilburn. However this arrangement was opposed and failed to obtain Parliamentary approval in the 1909 Session.

But 1909 was a significant year for one of London's main line railways, the London & North Western (LNWR), for it was in that year that it began work on a massive scheme to build two additional tracks between Watford Junction and Euston. The new lines were to be electrified, and the intention was to divert the majority of its suburban services on to the additional lines.

This section of the LNWR had been a part of the historic London & Birmingham Railway whose first section, between London and Boxmoor, had opened on 20th July 1837 (the remainder of that line opened the following year). When opened, the only passenger station between the terminus at Euston Square (over 17 miles away) and Watford was at Harrow. Initially trains were hauled by rope and winding engine between Euston and Camden Town because of the steep gradients, a practice which continued until 1844 – at about which time a station was opened at Camden Town. Amalgamation with a number of other companies in 1846 transformed the London & Birmingham Railway into the trunk portion of the London & North Western Railway, by which time a few additional intermediate stations had been added. Although goods and trunk passenger traffic developed (requiring four-tracking) the same enthusiasm was not shown towards local traffic and by the turn of the century only six further stations were added, together with a better-sited station at Watford Junction.

A little after the turn of the century the LNWR looked to developing its London local traffic. It was recognised that some of the areas through which its lines passed were not developing rapidly because of the absence of suitable stations and the limited suburban service. Inevitably the cost would be high because much of the existing route would require further (expensive) widening. The potential, however, was recognised.

The widening, and the new electrified railway scheme were announced in 1906. Starting from new platforms at Watford Junction the line would take over part of the existing Rickmansworth branch (opened 1862) and turn off just south of Watford High Street station to veer east to join and parallel the main line at Bushey. It would keep to the west side of the line as far as Wembley, where just south of the station it would pass underneath the main line to emerge on the east side as far as Willesden Junction, where a new station would be built a little way from the existing one. South of here the new line would remain on the east side to a point south of Kilburn where it would dive into large-diameter tube tunnels and run beneath the main line to serve underground stations at Loudoun Road and Chalk Farm. The line would then continue underground to Euston to serve a new platform built on an enormous reversing loop beneath the main line terminus. A number of new stations was envisaged on the new lines, in addition to which traffic from some of the existing stations would be switched, in part or in whole, to the new service. Powers for the scheme were obtained in 1907 but the finance was not immediately forthcoming and a start was delayed.

When work actually began on the LNWR's electric scheme in 1909 uncertainties were already arising about the expensive southern end of the route and the terminal arrangements at Euston. The LNWR therefore announced that work on the tube section would be left until last and that the finished sections could be worked by steam traction until the scheme was completed. Work proceeded accordingly. It was during the same year that the close relationship with the North London Railway was consummated when that railway was absorbed by the LNWR; this secured goods access to the Thames docks and pas-

The Bakerloo Line surfaces just south of Queen's Park station. This view shows the ramps under construction in 1914; just to their right new car sheds were built.

*London Transport Museum**

senger access to the City (Broad Street station) via either Kensal Rise and Hampstead Heath or a short link near Chalk Farm.

In 1911, when widening work was well advanced, the LNWR announced that the Euston loop proposal had been abandoned. A revised scheme was arrived at where instead of a single southern terminus there would now be three. City bound passengers would get a through electric service to Broad Street (via connections at Willesden and Chalk Farm), while West End passengers would get direct trains via a new tube line from Queen's Park, joining the Bakerloo Line at Paddington. Through Bakerloo Line trains would operate from Watford Junction to Elephant & Castle. The residue of the new service would operate to Euston main line via a junction at Chalk Farm (LNWR), the link to Euston being via existing tracks which would be electrified. The same announcement presaged the modernization and electrification of the North London Railway's western group of lines to Richmond and Kew, and the ˙NWR/UERL route from Willesden Junction to Earls Court. An LNWR Act of 1912 authorized the necessary junction works at Chalk Farm while an LER Act of the same year authorized an extension of the Bakerloo Line from Paddington to Queen's Park; work started in the autumn of 1912.

The Bakerloo link was to incorporate three new intermediate stations, to be built at Warwick Avenue (initially to have been called Warrington Crescent), Maida Vale and Kilburn Park.

The joint operation of the Watford line presumed that the Baker-loo Line had already reached Paddington, and this required separate parliamentary powers, granted in 1911. The 1906 route was re-arranged to allow for a northerly projection whilst retaining a good interchange with the Great Western and Metropolitan Railways. The earlier difficulties in achieving this were overcome by a pragmatic, if inelegant, formula in causing the extension to swing south after leaving Edgware Road and then to embark upon a huge, but never-theless sharp, curve which brought it back facing north-west. Work began in June 1911, and, after the LER 1912 Act was passed, was expanded to include the Queen's Park extension.

Although the original section of the Bakerloo Line remained sub-stantially unchanged while the thrust to the north-west was under way there were nevertheless a few improvements. The pre-opening reconstruction of Oxford Circus had been something of an unhappy compromise, and even by 1909 the arrangements were proving quite unsatisfactory and major changes were necessary (a problem to be echoed on the Underground ever since). Powers were obtained in the LER Act 1910 for the provision of additional low-level passages and a new below-street ticket hall, and a pair of escalators connecting the two. The new ticket hall and escalators came into partial use on 9th May 1914 and when the works were complete that part of the street level ticket hall not required for stairways was let for commercial use.

Another troublesome station was Embankment. The extension of the Hampstead Line from Charing Cross to Embankment in 1914 resulted in widespread changes and the excavation of a new concourse below the District Line tracks. Escalators were installed both for access to the new Hampstead Line platform and to those of the Bakerloo Line, replacing the original inclined subway. A new subway was also built to connect the Bakerloo and Hampstead Lines at low level. The District Line station entrance was rebuilt at the same time. It should be mentioned here that although these station names are the same as those used for the same locations today, this period saw several potentially confusing alterations (some of which were altered back in the 1970s). Thus from 6th April 1914 the Bakerloo Line sta-tion at Embankment was renamed 'Charing Cross (Embankment)', the Hampstead Line platforms there opening the same day and with the same name. The 'Embankment' suffix was dropped altogether from 9th May the following year, and the naming of the tube level platforms then accorded with the name of the District Railway sta-tion above. (From the same date the Hampstead's existing station at Charing Cross became 'Strand'.)

1914 was also the year when changes were made at Baker Street to improve the interchange with the Metropolitan Railway. Two escala-tors were introduced on 15th October 1914 to link the Bakerloo Line platforms with a new interchange concourse directly below the Metropolitan Railway's 'extension' platforms, that part of their station being rebuilt at about the same time. An interchange ticket office selling Metropolitan Railway tickets was opened in the new concourse. The Bakerloo's separate station in upper Baker Street, and some lifts, were retained.

The first section of the north-western extensions, the half-mile from Edgware Road to Paddington, had already opened by then, on 1st December 1913. At last the Great Western's terminus had a convenient link with central London, a privilege for which they contributed only some £18,000. The Bakerloo's new station was a fairly conventional layout at platform level, with two platforms (on a rather sharp curve) and crossover and reversing tunnels beyond. But it was unusual in one respect in being the first station on the line to open from new with the access from the surface not by lifts but by means of escalators (these had been successfully employed at Earls Court station the previous year), two being provided astride a fixed stairway. A sub-surface ticket hall was built, with stairways leading up to Praed Street and the main line station, and a subway connection with the existing passage linking the main line and Metropolitan Railway station.

The outbreak of the First World War, and other construction delays, meant the Bakerloo extension from Paddington to Queen's Park was not ready for opening until 31st January 1915. Trains ran empty between Kilburn Park and Queen's Park for a further ten days because the latter station was not quite ready (it opened on 11th February 1915) and even then the new facilities were not complete. Maida Vale station was also unfinished and could not be opened until 6th June 1915. At the low level the stations were similar, with platforms flanking a lower concourse from which a pair of escalators and a fixed stairway led to the ticket hall. Platform finishes were in green and white tiles with plasterwork ceiling. Warwick Avenue ticket hall was beneath the roadway and stairways led up to the edges of the pavement. At Maida Vale and Kilburn Park, single storey surface buildings finished in ruby-coloured glazed blocks were constructed, though at Maida Vale the ticket hall was actually at basement level.

At Queen's Park the existing station was reconstructed by the LNWR to provide for four additional platforms arranged as two islands. The outer faces of the island platforms were served (though not until 1922) by the LNWR local trains – from 1917 the former main line platforms closed to regular traffic. The inner faces of the island platforms were used by Bakerloo trains, which emerged from tube tunnel some quarter-mile to the south and thence ran in a steeply graded cutting to reach the level of the existing railway. A new twin-road car shed was build just to the south of the new plat-

A 1914 motor car built by Brush Engineering. These were of all-steel construction and embodied a centre door, though retaining the gated entrance as well. Similar (but not identical) cars were also built by Leeds Forge.   *'Electric Traction' A.T. Dover 1922*

forms, and to the north was a further car shed, of four roads. Curiously, the outer pair of roads through the north shed actually formed part of the new route to Watford, the junction with the new LNWR lines being immediately to the north of this shed. Neither shed was quite complete at the time the extension opened.

A new signal cabin was built at Queen's Park with a small power frame, although the signals on the LER lines were of the semaphore type controlled by electro-pneumatic motors. A new substation was constructed next to the passenger station at Kilburn Park, and power was supplied from Lots Road. In the same year, London Road substation at the southern end of the line was closed and replaced by a new one at Elephant & Castle, which also served the City & South London Railway.

Extension to Queen's Park stretched the line's provision of rolling stock. Initially, twelve new motor cars and two new trailers were ordered in 1914 which, together with a number of spare trailers of GNP&BR origin, allowed several new trains to be made up. Ten of the new motor cars were built by Brush, while the other four cars were built by Leeds Forge.

Some of the LNWR new lines had come into use even before the Bakerloo Line had reached Queen's Park. A new branch to Croxley Green from the junction with the Rickmansworth branch (near Watford High Street, which was reconstructed) came into use on 15th June 1912. On the same day the new lines from Harrow & Wealdstone to a point south of Willesden came into use, together with new stations at Kenton, North Wembley, Stonebridge Park and Harlesden (and the new platforms at Willesden Junction). The services were initially provided with steam-hauled trains and London services used the existing tracks to a point just north of Kensal Green tunnels, where a temporary junction and signal box were provided.

Between Watford High Street and Harrow the new lines came into use on 10th February 1913, together with an additional station at Headstone Lane and a new section of track (forming the third side of a triangle) from the Croxley/Rickmansworth branches towards Bushey. A station at Carpenders Park emerged on 1st April 1914, though it closed again from January 1917 until May 1919.

The new lines between Kensal Green tunnels and Queen's Park were ready from 10th May 1915, on which day a 15-minute Bakerloo Line service was projected northwards from Queen's Park to Willesden Junction where the trains reversed in the bay platforms.

View of the turbine room at the power station at Stonebridge Park, which supplied current to the LNWR's London electric services, including the Watford line.
LMS booklet describing the power station, 1933

The inauguration of this extension saw the first example of tube-sized rolling stock, in passenger service, sharing tracks and platforms used by main line trains, with attendant problems described later. The steam service to Watford continued to operate northwards, using the outer platforms at Willesden. Power was temporarily supplied from the Underground's Lots Road power station, as the LNWR's arrangements were not then ready. A new station at Kensal Green, initially served only by Bakerloo trains, came into use on 1st October 1916.

Although the North London Line electrification came into use in 1916 the completion of the full LNWR scheme was severely hampered by wartime restrictions and the work required for the complicated junctions at Chalk Farm where substantial widening was required. With all the flying junctions there were at one point no fewer than seventeen tracks at up to nine different levels, some climbing and some descending. However, from 16th April 1917 the new services were introduced so far as progress then allowed.

Bakerloo Line trains operated a weekdays only (and Sundays from 1919) service at about 15-minute intervals northwards to Watford Junction, and the LNWR provided an electric service from Watford to Broad Street via Hampstead Heath. The steam service continued to operate between Euston and Watford Junction via the new lines, and this was augmented by an additional steam service which plied non-stop between Euston and the new platforms at Willesden, where it connected with the electric trains.

Full services were introduced in 1922 following completion of the works at Chalk Farm. Electric trains now operated from Watford to Euston, Watford to Broad Street via Hampstead Heath, Watford to Broad Street via Primrose Hill (as Chalk Farm had become), and Watford to Elephant & Castle via the Bakerloo Line. In 1923 a reversing siding was commissioned at Harrow.

The LNWR had constructed its own power station at Stonebridge Park, which came into use early in 1916 and eventually supplied power to most of its London d.c. services. Current was generated at 11,000 volts, 25 cycles per second, and was transmitted to the various substations, six of which were on the Queen's Park–Watford portion (at Bushey, Headstone Lane, Kenton, Stonebridge Park, Willesden and Queen's Park). Adjacent to the power station was the main workshop for the LNWR's new electric services and all their new stock was maintained there. In addition, a new running depot was built near Croxley Green, and this was used for stabling and minor maintenance of both LNWR and Underground stock. The LNWR also had a minor maintenance and stabling shed at Mitre Bridge, Willesden. Signalling on the new lines was mechanically-operated, controlled generally from new signal cabins distinct from those supervising the main lines.

For the Bakerloo's Watford service it had been the intention for the LNWR and LER to purchase new stock jointly, and an order was placed with the Metropolitan Carriage, Wagon & Finance Company in 1915 for 72 new tube cars. Unfortunately the prevailing war made it quite impossible for the carbuilders to meet this order at this time. However, 24 new motor cars happened to be in course of delivery to the Central London Railway to service the Ealing extension, itself delayed by wartime priorities. These temporarily surplus motor cars were thus put into service on the Bakerloo Line with ex-GNP&BR gate stock trailers. Together they provided the mainstay of the Watford service for about four years, though the motor bogies on the Central London cars did not take kindly to the high speed running to Watford and had to be replaced.

This exigency was not entirely without problems, because the platforms north of Queen's Park had been built to main line height and there would have been a very considerable step down into ordinary tube cars. Interestingly, in 1911 the Underground Group had been considering the problems of running tube trains through main line height platforms, and had even indulged in some experiments with tube stock on the South Acton–South Harrow service (then part of the Metropolitan District Railway, with full height platforms). The Board of Trade was somewhat alarmed at the makeshift arrangement of hinged and slideable steps fitted to cars upon which the public had been let loose. They declined to approve the arrangement, suspecting something similar might be used on the Watford service for which powers were then being sought.

What actually emerged on the Bakerloo's Watford trains was even more makeshift. Trains were made up of five cars, the middle three of which were of gate stock trailers. The end vestibules of these cars were fitted with a modified floor where the edges adjacent to the station platforms were raised by some $4^{1}/2$ inches, this being a compromise between a tube height and a main line height platform. Unfortunately the new motor cars had enclosed end vestibules where it was not possible to raise the floor because passengers might then bang their heads on the roof. North of Queen's Park they had to negotiate what was perceived as the lesser evil of the 10-inch step between car and platform as best they could. The LER subsequently stated that they only acceded to the pressure to begin the Watford service in 1917, before they were ready, because of the LNWR's severe locomotive shortage.

The Joint Stock eventually arrived in 1920, in the form of 36 motor cars, 24 trailers and 12 control trailers, designed to produce 12 6-car trains (most of the trains other than those providing the Watford service were of five cars). For the first time there was a motor car in the centre of the formation, and special dispensation was granted

One of the early Watford service trains just south of Watford High Street, on a trial run prior to the commencement of public operation. The leading car is one of the Central London Railway motor cars loaned to the Bakerloo, as is the last car, while the intermediate three are gate stock trailers on loan from the Piccadilly and fitted with temporary steps.

London Transport Museum*

by the Board of Trade once a number of additional safety precautions had been complied with. The car floors were a little higher than on other tube stock, which minimised the step up at the LNWR stations. The Joint Stock was maintained by the Underground Group although several trains were stabled at Croxley Green. The LER owned only 24 of the cars, the LNWR owning the rest.

For the Watford–Euston and Broad Street services the LNWR ordered in 1921 thirty 3-car sets of open saloon stock fitted with Oerlikon electrical equipment; these were similar to batches delivered in 1914/15 for other services. In the later 1920s some additional, compartment stock sets were supplied, fitted with GEC or British Thomson-Houston equipment.

One final result of the First World War, whose main effect for the Bakerloo Line was of delays and increasing costs for the northwestern extension, was to raise fears for the security of the Bakerloo's under-river tunnels. At one point these are only three feet below the River Thames. Although nothing permanent was done during the war itself these sections of tunnel received a secondary steel protective lining during 1919/20. This subsequently proved troublesome and part of it was removed during the Second World War, with tremendous inconvenience.

29

A Watford Joint Stock trailer car, photographed at Lillie Bridge. This was the first Bakerloo Line stock to have enclosed end platforms, though the doors were still operated by gatemen using a hand lever. The centre door was unlocked by one of the gatemen. On the motor cars one of the gate ends was replaced by the driving cab, motor bogie and equipment compartment.   *London Transport Museum**

The Underground continued to expand in the 1920s. Early priority was given to completion of pre-war extension schemes, and to enlargement and modernization of major stations in central London. The Bakerloo Line benefited from station reconstruction. Waterloo station was enlarged between 1924 and 1927 as part of the works for extending the Hampstead Line southwards from Charing Cross to Kennington. A flight of three escalators linked a new ticket hall area beneath the main line station with a low-level concourse serving both the Hampstead and Bakerloo Lines, although the existing Bakerloo lifts and ticket hall were retained.

At Charing Cross (now Embankment) the booking hall area was significantly enlarged and a new booking office opened on 6th December 1920; new subways were also built to provide better access to the tube from street level. Additional enlargements were also made in 1926 when the Hampstead Line was extended southwards from Charing Cross to Kennington. 1926 was also a significant year at Trafalgar Square where on 13th April a pair of escalators replaced the existing lifts, though the original ticket hall was retained and modernized.

The biggest modernization was at Piccadilly Circus where the existing lifts and low-level passages were replaced by escalators. A lower flight of three escalators served just the Bakerloo Line, while another flight of three served the Piccadilly Line. These six escalators converged at an intermediate level which was connected to ticket hall level by means of a further flight of five escalators (in two shafts). The ticket hall was a vast, elliptical area built directly beneath Piccadilly Circus itself. The escalators emerged in the centre of the ticket hall, from the perimeter of which six subways and staircases brought passengers in from various street corners. One of these connected with the old station building which was retained to provide three further street entrances.

Interior of Watford Joint Stock car, 1920.   *London Transport Museum**

Work began in February 1925 with the sinking of a service shaft, requiring the temporary removal of the Shaftesbury Memorial (Eros) which occupied the surface working site. Much of the construction work involved the diversion of the utility service mains, for which purpose a large pipe subway had to be driven around the ticket hall site before the main excavation could begin. The new station was designed by Charles Holden & Partners, and when completed the interior finishings of the new ticket hall were luxurious and distinctly *art deco* in flavour. The new ticket hall, escalators and passageways were opened on 10th December 1928 by the Mayor of Westminster.

Increasing central London traffic quickly outgrew the modernized, but still cramped, facilities at Oxford Circus station, which again featured as a bottleneck. In 1923 work had begun once more to provide additional facilities. This time the Bakerloo's sub-surface ticket hall was extended below Argyll and Oxford Streets to incorporate escalators leading to the Central London Railway, and this work was ready for opening on 5th July 1925; the Central London's street level building was reduced to providing additional stairway entrances to the enlarged below-street ticket hall. A little later a third Bakerloo Line escalator was added, in a separate shaft, and this came into use in November 1928, allowing the older Bakerloo escalators to be modernized, one at a time.

31

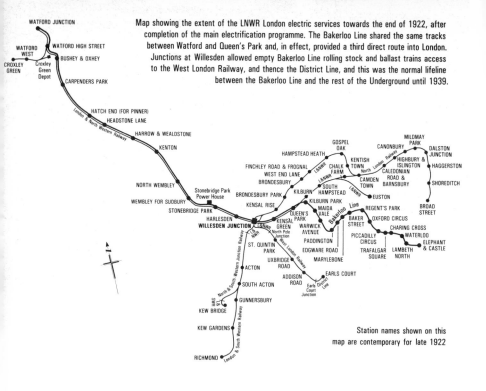

Map showing the extent of the LNWR London electric services towards the end of 1922, after completion of the main electrification programme. The Bakerloo Line shared the same tracks between Watford and Queen's Park and, in effect, provided a third direct route into London. Junctions at Willesden allowed empty Bakerloo Line rolling stock and ballast trains access to the West London Railway, and thence the District Line, and this was the normal lifeline between the Bakerloo Line and the rest of the Underground until 1939.

Station names shown on this map are contemporary for late 1922

    The late 1920s was a period when the Underground was once more expanding, and the extension and modernization of the Piccadilly Line is the most obvious result visible today. South London had not fared well in the Underground's expansion programme but considerable pressure was repeatedly brought for a south London tube to serve areas not adequately dealt with by the Southern Railway, which had embarked on wholesale electrification of its suburban lines. One such scheme, endorsed by a public inquiry held by the London & Home Counties Traffic Advisory Committee in 1926, was for a Bakerloo extension to Camberwell, but the UERL was unconvinced and nothing was done. However in 1930, thanks to government-financed cheap capital funds for schemes to relieve unemployment, the extension became viable, as had the Piccadilly Line scheme. Parliamentary powers were obtained in 1931. The extension was to be 1³/4 miles (2.8km) long, with stations at Albany Road and Denmark Hill; Elephant & Castle station was to be reconstructed. Unfortunately the rapidly deteriorating financial position of the UERL made a start impossible, though the powers were kept alive and some detailed planning was undertaken.

Although a posed photograph, this view of a gate stock train at Elephant & Castle clearly illustrates the arrangement of entrances between adjacent cars. The gateman, who operated both the platform gates and the car doors at each pair of platforms, may be seen standing between the cars. *London Transport Museum**

In the same period the Bakerloo Line found itself with an embarrassing problem on its hands with regard to its rolling stock. In contrast to the modernized stations, even in the mid 1920s, about two-thirds of the Bakerloo Line's in-town service, from Queen's Park to Elephant & Castle, was still provided by relatively antiquated and highly staff-intensive gate stock, mainly of 1906 vintage, with a few more modern cars of 1914 origin. A similar problem was to be found on several other tube lines. A line by line programme of gate stock replacement was authorized to improve train services.

The Hampstead Line had begun introducing an improved style of train in 1923, using all-steel cars based on the best of a number of sample cars made by different manufacturers. After further refinement a batch of similar cars was ordered for the Bakerloo, where the last gate stock train ran on the night of 31st December 1929. The 182 new cars were built by the Union Construction & Finance Company at premises in Feltham, which company was a subsidiary of the UERL; consequently the cars were often referred to as Felthams. This particular order was shared with the Piccadilly Line, and to complicate matters further some cars from the Hampstead Line's 1926/7 deliveries were also transferred to the Bakerloo. 6-car trains were now operated on the in-town service.

Standard stock provided the mainstay of the Bakerloo Line service from about 1928 to 1941, with a handful of trains lasting a few years more. The train shown here is southbound at what is now Wembley Central and is of the Watford Replacement Stock batch, dedicated to use on the Watford service. These trains carried a blue stripe along the cream upper panels to indicate their description to passengers. *London Transport Museum**

A further batch of cars ordered in 1930 was known as the Watford Replacement Stock, being ordered from Metropolitan Cammell as a direct substitute for the Joint Stock cars, most of which were scrapped. These cars had proved slow and not satisfactory and could not easily be adapted for air-door operation. The replacement cars were generally similar to the Felthams but incorporated electro-pneumatic brakes and 'weak field' motor control, features which assisted with the higher speeds operated north of Queen's Park. The new carbodies had normal Underground height floor levels, requiring the platform heights north of Queen's Park to be adjusted to a 'compromise' between main line and tube requirements.

The London, Midland & Scottish Railway (LMS), which had inherited the lines north of Queen's Park in 1923, retained a number of its Joint Stock cars and for some years they were used to operate the Rickmansworth and Croxley Green branches. In 1932/3 all the semaphore signals on the Euston–Watford new line were replaced by a unique coloured light system using searchlight signals and electrically operated trainstops. Signal cabins were only retained where there were points or junctions which, together with shunt signals, continued to be operated mechanically. The LMS and ex-LNWR trains were equipped with tripcocks in connection with the new signalling, the Bakerloo trains already having them.

By July 1932, 32 6-car trains were being operated on the Bakerloo Line, with 15 trains (and a spare) on the Watford service and 15 (and a spare) on the in-town service. This provided a $2^1/2$-minute frequency south of Queen's Park, and a roughly $7^1/2$-minute interval of Bakerloo trains between Harrow and Queen's Park with alternate trains originating from Watford Junction. The same intervals were maintained throughout the midday off-peak, though only by 3-car trains.

Between June 1932 and 1937 trains on the Bakerloo's Watford service had a wide blue stripe painted along the carbodies which differentiated them from the 'local' trains – destination indicators on Bakerloo Line platforms not being fitted until after the Second World War. From 1932 enhanced Watford services required additional 'Watford' cars, which were obtained by modifying ordinary cars re-allocated from other lines. From the late 1930s much of the older (and all new) tube stock was fitted with electro-pneumatic brakes, brake retarders and weak field control, and it was no longer necessary to have a specialized fleet for use north of Queen's Park.

One point of interest concerns the interworking of tube and main line trains in the event of a failure. Normally if a railway train fails completely then arrangements are made for another train to push or pull the defective train out of the way. But if some trains were tube height and some were main line height the different coupling arrangements prevented their assisting each other. In Watford Joint Stock days the ruling was that in the event of failure non-compatible trains had to be got out of the way to enable a similar train to help out. Nevertheless, a steam locomotive could help a tube train by means of a special 'match' wagon which was kept available.

When the Watford Replacement Stock was delivered a more flexible arrangement was arrived at. This stock could be fitted with what is best described as a rigid towbar and a removable floor mounting, both of which were stowed away beneath train seats until needed. If one of these tube trains became disabled, and the following train was of main line electric stock, the equipment could be fitted in order to enable the main line train to assist the tube (the reverse was not allowed). This arrangement was continued – at least in theory – until the early 1980s.

After years of public debate, an entirely new type of public corporation came into existence on 1st July 1933. This was the London Passenger Transport Board (LPTB), which took control of London's bus, tramway and Underground systems. At the same time, a standing joint committee of the LPTB and the four main line railway companies was formed; within the new Board's area the joint committee was responsible for the fares levels of all the transport concerns, together with planning policy for passenger services.

By far the largest component of the Board's acquisitions was the UERL and its transport subsidiaries, among which was the LER's Bakerloo Line. It is therefore not surprising that the LPTB installed itself in the UERL's headquarters building – Holden's impressive block referred to as 55 Broadway. Nor is it surprising that most of the senior managers originated from the UERL, including Lord Ashfield who, many years previously as Albert Stanley, had worked on the early tube lines. There was not, therefore, any dramatic change in direction in management style.

Much of the justification for the new body was the opportunity provided for substantial and co-ordinated improvements to London's public transport facilities. Within two years a massive programme of investment was launched, which became known as the 1935–40 New Works Programme. It was to have a profound effect on the future of the Bakerloo Line, though the actual changes – substantial by any scale – were less dramatic than originally envisaged.

When the initial list of New Works projects was compiled (in 1934) a £30–35 million estimate allowed for a large range of schemes, including the one previously dropped from the unemployment relief programme – the Camberwell extension. Unfortunately rapidly increasing estimates, coupled with even greater outside pressures for extensions in north London, meant that Camberwell did not feature in the scheme put before the Treasury in 1935, though powers were kept alive and the extension featured in later plans for a possible 1940–50 New Works Programme (including possible extension beyond Camberwell over the Southern Railway to Dartford, or the proposed new airport at Lullingstone). Two short sidings and a crossover were built at Elephant & Castle using the parliamentary powers granted for the Camberwell extension, and came into use around 1940 to assist train handling at the Elephant terminus. Meanwhile the central London section of the Bakerloo Line, south from Baker Street, found a major new role thrust upon it in the 1935–40 Programme.

The LPTB had inherited a substantial 'Underground' railway not historically part of the UERL group. This was the Metropolitan Railway whose 'extension' lines out of Baker Street served the northwest quadrant of outer London and Middlesex, and meandered into Hertfordshire and deepest Buckinghamshire. Included in this inheritance was a major bottleneck caused by the numerous branches all feeding into a main stem. South from Harrow parallel pairs of fast and slow tracks combined by means of a flat junction at Finchley Road into just two tracks through 2-mile twin tunnels to Baker Street. In this latter section were three intermediate stations, at Swiss Cottage, Marlborough Road and St. John's Wood (later known as Lord's). Traffic was burgeoning as the outer suburbs developed rapidly, and the combination of just two tracks, a flat junction and local stations proved a major problem.

A scheme had been devised in 1926 where a line would be thrown off near Kilburn and drop down into a tube tunnel beneath the Edgware Road to join the Circle Line at Edgware Road station, but apart from the rebuilding of the latter nothing else was done. In a desperate attempt to ease the congestion, Marlborough Road and St. John's Wood stations were closed during the rush hours from 1929. While this helped the trains to a limited extent it did nothing for local passengers who were deprived of a station at the very time they most wanted to use it, and the practice gradually ceased.

Another answer had to be found for this mounting problem. By the time the LPTB took over matters were made worse by the opening of the Stanmore branch in 1932. This diverged from the main line just north of Wembley Park station and added to the conflict at Wembley Park where, in effect, the 'fast' lines crossed the 'slow' lines on the level.

The solution adopted by the LPTB fulfilled three objectives. firstly it utilized some of the potential spare capacity of the Bakerloo Line south of Baker Street; the prevailing 24 trains per hour Bakerloo peak service could be increased to at least 32, it was considered, with fewer trains serving the Queen's Park–Paddington section. Secondly it provided the Metropolitan Line with a much desired direct access to the West End from many suburban stations, and a cross-platform service from all the others. Thirdly it alleviated the problems of the Finchley Road–Baker Street bottleneck.

The solution was met by forming a junction with the Bakerloo Line at Baker Street and building a new tube branch with local stations to meet up with the Metropolitan Line at Finchley Road; Bakerloo trains would then be projected northwards over Metropolitan Line tracks. Irrespective of whose trains they were and how the improvements were sold to the public, the works can most accurately be viewed as a continuation of the Metropolitan's four-tracking southwards to Baker Street and extending (tube size) Metropolitan trains through the West End via the Bakerloo. The relevant parliamentary powers were obtained in 1935.

Work began in April 1936 and was pushed ahead quickly. Twin tube tunnels diverged from the Metropolitan Line station at Finchley Road, which was completely rebuilt. The tubes dived down steeply to a point near Swiss Cottage station where new tube platforms were constructed linked by escalators to a new booking hall below the road intersection and contiguous with the Metropolitan Line station which was to remain open. Southwards below the Finchley Road the tubes continued towards a new station called St. John's Wood, halfway between Marlborough Road and St. John's Wood (Metropolitan) which were to be closed for regular use.

At Baker Street, the new southbound line emerged into a new southbound Bakerloo platform which, together with the existing one (from Queen's Park), straddled a new concourse area from which two escalators carried passengers up to an enlargement of the existing interchange concourse under the Metropolitan Line. No additional platform was built for the northbound branch traffic, the junction being north of the existing platform. A new ticket hall was also built at street level for easier access to the Bakerloo Line, at the corner of upper Baker Street and Marylebone Road. It was linked both to the existing Metropolitan Line ticket hall, and, by a pair of escalators, to the enlarged interchange concourse under the Metropolitan Line platforms. The original Bakerloo ticket hall and lifts in upper Baker Street survived until after the Second World War, though they were little used.

North of Finchley Road substantial changes were made to the existing infrastructure. Extensive track re-arrangement and signalling modernization was undertaken with revised directions of running and some flying junctions. Most stations were altered to some extent and some were completely reconstructed. A vast modern depot was built at Neasden (on the site of the old Metropolitan Railway works) which eventually became the main maintenance facility for both the Metropolitan and the Bakerloo Lines.

It was not until 2nd November 1939 that Bakerloo trains began operating between Stanmore and Elephant & Castle. Under the new arrangements the Stanmore branch service was entirely handed over to Bakerloo Line trains, as was the most of the local service between Wembley Park and Finchley Road. South of Baker Street resignalling allowed Bakerloo Line services to be considerably intensified, to about 36 per hour in the peaks, with about half the trains originating from the Stanmore branch.

The original signals had been altered from the moving spectacle type to 2-aspect coloured light type by the mid 1920s, but the signalling layouts had not otherwise been substantially modernized. From about 1938 the automatic signalling was progressively altered and brought up to the then prevailing standard, while the signalling south of Baker Street allowed for the intensified service. New signal cabins were brought into use at Elephant & Castle, Lambeth North and Baker Street, while new or rebuilt power-frames were provided at Paddington and Queen's park. A new signal cabin was also built at

Piccadilly Circus, replacing the first cabin which had come into operation a few years after the line had opened. At both Piccadilly Circus and Lambeth North the trailing crossovers were replaced by scissors crossovers. (By then the cabins at Edgware Road and Marylebone had been removed).

Platform lengthening had become urgent to increase passenger capacity. The Bakerloo had inherited platforms, each nominally 290 feet (88m) long, from pre-Yerkes days. Because each 6-car train carried two equipment compartments the length of train actually available for passengers was only $5^1/3$ cars. On this basis the early intention to extend to 8-car long platforms with traditional trains with an intermediate motor car would increase the effective passenger space to 7-cars.

However, before any work was done, the viability of a new type of train had been proved. This innovative train became known as the 1938 stock and differed from its predecessors in having all the control equipment below the floor. By this means the whole of the car interiors (except for the driving cabs) was available for passenger use. If at least some 1938 stock were used on the Bakerloo Line then platform extension to seven cars length was all that was necessary. It was decided to use the new style trains on the busier (Paddington) branch to mitigate the effect of the reduced train service which would inevitably result when part of the service was switched to Stanmore (in fact during the peak hour slightly more than half the service ran from the Queen's Park branch).

The platform extension work was complicated because it took place at the end of platforms which were in daily use, and around existing running tunnels. Where possible only one end of a platform was extended but site conditions sometimes required short extensions at both ends. The work was severely delayed during the war and the extensions were not put into use until 1946. The whole line, including the Queen's Park and Watford services, had to put up with 6-car trains until then.

The 1938 stock initially entered service on the Northern Line from June 1938, but from late 1939 6-car 1938 stock trains began to enter service on the Bakerloo (spare cars, to make the trains up to 7-cars, were temporarily stored). A number of the new trains were available at the time the Stanmore branch opened.

The pre-war intention was for the Bakerloo to be run by a pool of 135 cars (7-car trains plus spare motor cars) of pre-1938 stock and 224 cars (32 7-car trains) of 1938 stock, including 52 (later 58) trailer cars of older stock – with no control equipment above floor – converted to work with the new trains. The former would operate in 7-car formations on the Stanmore service while the latter higher capacity trains would operate on the busier Queen's Park and Watford service. To a large extent this initially happened, and by January 1940 some 28 of the line's 45 trains were of 1938 stock, including the entire Queen's Park–Watford service of 25 trains.

However, in these troubled times events finally turned out different from the plan. A substantial mileage of the Northern Line's extensions had been curtailed during the war and there were therefore many 1938 stock cars temporarily surplus to requirements. Meanwhile the new cars on the Bakerloo had not run well with the old stock because of their different operating characteristics – the new trains kept catching up the older ones.

The decision then came to be made to put as much as possible of the spare 1938 stock into Bakerloo service in preference to old stock which was stored instead. As the new trains were of higher capacity and the platform lengthening work had been delayed by the war, this move made sense for other reasons too. By 1946 there were only five old stock trains still running on the Bakerloo. Following completion of platform lengthening in the same year the stored 1938 stock cars were introduced into the new trains lengthening them to 7-cars.

After the war it became evident that the remaining Northern Line extensions would never be completed – the 1938 stock 'temporarily' running on the Bakerloo could remain there. This decision had its problems in that while the bulk of the 1938 stock was intended to run in 7-car formations, some trains on the Northern Line had originally been intended to run in 6-car and 9-car formations, and the mix of cars had been ordered accordingly. The requirement to press as many new trains into service as possible had exhausted the mix of cars required to produce the standard 7-car trains, although a few additional 7-car trains had emerged using non-standard combinations.

What was left were some 41 modern cars which were virtually unusable in their existing form. To use these cars there was a further revision to 1938 stock allocations, permitting more 7-car trains though with more non-standard formations. Most of these changes had taken place by 1949. A later move was the construction of some 91 new cars (the 1949 stock) which allowed the existing fleet to be standardized (mopping up odd cars) as well as creating yet further trains. The 1949 cars were of two types, of which 21 were trailers and the balance non-driving motor cars incorporating a new feature – a simplified driving control panel locked behind an end panel and used purely for shunting purposes (this reduced the cost compared with normal driving motors). The new cars were eventually distributed amongst the 1938 stock fleet on the Northern, Bakerloo and Piccadilly Lines, and the remarshalling task was completed by 1954.

Following the reconstruction of Piccadilly Circus in 1928 the Bakerloo had to wait some time for further station improvements. As

Looking slightly lost, a 1938 stock train arrives at Watford Junction in 1977. In the adjacent platform is a 1957-built British Rail d.c. electric train, and the substantial variation in car floor heights is obvious, as is the utility of the 'compromise' height platform.   *John Glover*

a 1937 scheme (independent of the New Works Programme) it had been proposed at Marylebone to replace the existing three lifts with a pair of escalators which would lead directly up to the main line station concourse, where much of the traffic interchanged. The existing Underground station had the ticket hall at basement level from which there was a subway to the main line concourse. Work started before the war and could not well be abandoned in wartime conditions as the shaft was partly completed and lay in water-bearing ground. The work was therefore pursued on a temporary basis and the escalators and temporary ticket office on the main line concourse opened on 1st February 1943. As is sometimes the way, the 'temporary' surface structure, of pre-cast blocks, scaffolding and corrugated iron, survived until very recently when a new ticket office, selling both Underground and British Rail tickets, opened in December 1988.

After the war the government embarked on a massive programme of nationalization. The 1947 Transport Act led on 1st January 1948 to most of Britain's inland surface transport systems passing into the control of the British Transport Commission (BTC). The Underground (as with the rest of the LPTB) became part of the BTC, though much of the day to day control of the former LPTB operations was delegated to a subsidiary body, the London Transport Executive (LT). In a further change of events the BTC was abolished at the end of 1962 and London Transport passed to a new Board directly responsible to the Minister of Transport.

41

By 1948 the level of service scheduled on the trunk section of line south of Baker Street had increased to 36 trains per hour, and this was the maximum service level practicable. One of the main factors which made it difficult to improve services further was the simple, two-platform layout at Elephant & Castle. As it was, the turnaround time for trains here was about two minutes. This was insufficient to allow incoming traincrews to walk back along the platform, and required a process called 'stepping back', where there were more crews than trains at Elephant & Castle and the incoming crew took a later train away. The time was right to consider either an improved terminal arrangement with three platforms, or to examine once more the proposed Camberwell extension for which the powers still survived and which were once more renewed in 1948.

After much local agitation Lord Latham, the Chairman of LT from 1948, announced that the 1½-mile extension would be undertaken. The improved reversing facilities at Camberwell Green would allow an increase in service levels throughout the line, so LT proposed to purchase an additional 14 trains, which would in turn need a new depot, to be built at Stanmore. The whole scheme would cost about £4.5m. It was anticipated that work would begin in 1950 and would take about three years.

These extra facilities, though made possible by the improved terminal arrangements, sowed the seeds of destruction for the scheme. More detailed evaluations prior to the tendering process showed that the project would cost nearly over £6m and could not possibly be afforded in the prevailing financial climate. Money would not be forthcoming from the government, and the financial position of the BTC was steadily worsening. More relevantly, the huge post-war traffic increases on the Underground had levelled off and, if anything, had begun their long decline. The immediate pressure for improving terminal facilities for traffic purposes had abated – there was little other crucial need for the extension. The 1940 twin tunnels south of Elephant & Castle, utilized as sidings, remain as a memorial to the Camberwell extension.

Pre-war normality resumed on the Bakerloo Line from June 1950 when full length trains ceased to run during the slack periods; 3-car portions of trains were stabled, leaving 4-car trains in service. This gave rise to some difficulties at Watford where the 3-car portion had to be driven via Watford High Street to Croxley Green depot. The arrival of 1949 stock meant that the stabling portion was driven on passenger lines from a 'shunting' control panel within the passenger saloon. This proved unpopular and caused stock to be re-allocated so that fifteen normal 3-car units were available for use on the trains due to uncouple at Watford.

From December 1949 passenger door control had been introduced on the open sections of the Bakerloo Line; this was a pre-war idea which had not been entirely satisfactory, and the equipment was much modified as a result of the earlier experiences. The idea was that out of the rush hours passengers could open the doors adjacent to them from push buttons next to those doors (under the overriding control of the guard); this cut down wear and tear on doors through which no-one wished to board, and in cold weather helped to keep the cars warm. Neither passenger door control nor uncoupling proved sufficiently advantageous to outweigh the operational and maintenance complications which then resulted. They were abandoned respectively in 1959 and 1961.

At Waterloo the Festival of Britain activities on the South Bank brought heavy additional traffic to the Waterloo area and in anticipation of this a bank of three escalators was built from the lower tube station level to a new ticket hall near the exhibition site; these opened in May 1951. A few years later the construction of the Shell Building near the top of this shaft gave the opportunity for LT to construct a new permanent ticket hall at street level beneath the new building, and two of the three 'exhibition' escalators were utilized (the centre escalator had been removed for use at Green Park and a staircase substituted). The entrance was closed for reconstruction in 1957 and the new ticket hall opened in 1962. Charing Cross station also received attention during the Festival of Britain works, and two new escalators were provided to link the ticket hall level with the interchange concourse to the Bakerloo and Northern Lines.

During the 1950s the conditions at Oxford Circus station deteriorated to the extent that the station was frequently closed during the evening rush hour because of excessive congestion within the lower reaches of the station. Despite alterations to the passageways to the Bakerloo Line the layout was still quite inadequate. Even a pair of high-speed lifts was installed in 1942 to supplement the escalator service and ease matters, but conditions were most unsatisfactory. Reconstruction had been contemplated for some years but nothing was done post-war because of the emerging scheme for the Victoria Line, whose construction via Oxford Circus would of itself require massive changes.

Although powers were granted in 1955, government authority for the Victoria Line only arrived in August 1962; within a few weeks work began on the enormous task of reconstructing Oxford Circus station. What emerged was a vast new circular ticket hall underneath the 'circus' itself, with entrances in each quadrant to both sides of each street. From this ticket hall four escalators led to an intermediate level from where two pairs of escalators led to Bakerloo Line level (one pair to each platform). These latter escalators also served the Victoria Line when it opened, and were largely used to carry 'Way

In' traffic. The existing three Bakerloo Line escalators and the old ticket hall were retained and used exclusively to carry 'Way Out' traffic. Most of the old low-level subways were swept away and replaced with new passages mainly carrying one-way flows. New interchange passages to the Central Line were built. The new ticket hall was opened in 1968, and this section of the Victoria Line opened on 7th March 1969.

During 1957/58, while the go-ahead for the Victoria Line had still been awaited, planners had taken a further look at the future options for tube extensions south of the River. For practical purposes these were a continuation south from Victoria, or the Bakerloo Line beyond Elephant & Castle. In the latter case it was felt that a natural route for the Bakerloo would be towards what was then north Kent, but this would attract more traffic than the overcrowded central section of the Bakerloo Line could cope with and a more modest extension was all that could be accommodated.

Brixton was considered a reasonable objective, either for the Victoria Line or for the Bakerloo Line extended via Camberwell (for which there was still some moral commitment). In the end it was clear that the most justifiable extension on traffic, revenue and cost grounds was that of the Victoria Line, which reached Brixton in 1971. Parliamentary powers for Camberwell were allowed to lapse in 1961.

Perversely it was not long after abandoning parliamentary powers that new circumstances made a southwards Bakerloo extension a serious proposition again. In 1964 the joint LT and BR Passenger Transport Planning Committee for London desired that the route continued to be studied "but not as a task of first priority". By now a further limited extension beyond Camberwell to Peckham Rye was being considered; the thinking being that part of the justification for the extension could be rationalization and relief of overcrowding on sections of BR's Southern Region services. Later studies confirmed the desirability of such an extention and reiterated the unsatisfactory terminal at Elephant & Castle. The route was felt worth physically safeguarding.

The case for a southern extension became stronger in the late 1960s. Firstly, there was an LT Fleet Line project, described below, to relieve the central London sections of the Bakerloo of its worst overcrowding, which would in turn create more capacity for an extension beyond Camberwell. Secondly, after the 1963 London Government Act which two years later created the various London Boroughs and the Greater London Council, local boroughs had stronger and louder voices to argue their case. Southwark, once it had settled in, was pressing LT for an extension into the borough. As a result, in 1969, a joint working party between Southwark and LT was established to develop the Peckham proposal further. The transfer of London Transport to local political control in the form of the GLC from 1st January 1970 was another factor favouring examination of this type of extension. Finally government grants were available following the 1968 Transport Act which potentially covered up to 75 per cent of capital costs of such schemes.

A Peckham extension was thus viewed by all interested parties as a 'nice to have' railway – providing central government was willing to pay for it. As quickly as November 1970 it was viewed as one of the next logical moves after the Fleet Line and the Piccadilly Line extension to Heathrow. By 1972 Peckham was being included in the GLC's ambitious 20-year plans, and in LT's 10-year capital estimates.

By 1974 detailed planning had been undertaken and precise estimates made. However, while the extension would undoubtedly have improved transport facilities in the area, the cost/benefit analysis was unconvincing. Even with capital costs paid the line would run not produce a very worthwhile return because so much traffic would be siphoned off existing services. In other words the money would probably be better spent on something else.

In the absence of any compelling reason to proceed with the line urgently it was agreed to refer the scheme to the London Rail Study, and parliamentary powers were not sought immediately. The Rail Study reported in November 1974 and did not favour the extension to Peckham, labelling it as a "weak case" in planning as well as transport terms. It became clear that it would not be a high priority for government money, while tube railway schemes which had a higher GLC priority such as a Fleet Line extension were not favoured with central government support.

A further nail in the Peckham coffin was London Transport's proposal for an extensive network of 'Speedbuses' along roads with exclusive bus lanes, one route of which would serve Peckham. The speedbus produced most of the social benefit with little of the costs of a new railway. Bakerloo extension southwards was therefore forgotten and route safeguarding was abandoned. Speedbus did not happen either.

Once again the main Bakerloo developments transpired north of the Thames. After a 55-year gap between the opening of the Hampstead Tube across central London in 1907 and the Victoria Line authorization in 1962, specific proposals had been rapidly put forward by LT for another central London tube railway, intended to run east—west beneath Fleet Street and thence towards south-east London. This came to be called the Fleet Line, referred to earlier. Its ancestry goes back to a number of pre-Second World War and wartime railway schemes, but a more immediate cause was the problem of the inadequate services which were all that could be pro-

London Road depot viewed from above the tunnel mouth in 1983. A 1959 stock train is threading its way into the depot and two 1938 stock trains may be seen in the background. The photograph captures the semi-derelict air which pervaded the depot post-war. The car sheds (where the 1938 stock trains are stabled) have already been demolished having lain roofless for some years. The paint shop (the large building on the right) is virtually derelict and no longer rail connected. All the buildings except the covered pit roads on the far left were demolished in 1986.

John Glover

vided on the northern branches of the Bakerloo Line so long as they both converged on Baker Street.

The 1939 Stanmore service had in some respects transferred the Metropolitan Line's problems to the tube services below. It was not reliably possible to offer much more than a 4-minute interval service on either branch, and traffic levels demanded better, particularly to Paddington. Similarly, the section of Bakerloo Line south of Baker Street was heavily overcrowded and some sort of relief was required. This need became acute once cross-platform interchange existed with the Victoria Line at Oxford Circus.

Numerous options were considered, including the takeover of the Queen's Park branch by a new line, or a new direct tube line from Paddington to the West End instead of the more circuitous route via Baker Street. In the event, the Fleet Line project addressed these problems by duplicating the Bakerloo Line between Baker Street and Trafalgar Square (but via Bond Street and Green Park) and by taking over the Stanmore branch. The Bakerloo would thus revert to its pre-

1939 state with the main service running from Elephant & Castle to Queen's Park with some trains projected to Watford. LT's new masters were anxious to proceed with the Fleet Line and with the GLC meeting 25 per cent of the capital cost a first stage was authorized. This would produce a 'new' railway from Stanmore, via Baker Street, to its own terminal platforms at Charing Cross station, providing low-level interchange with the Bakerloo Line (at Trafalgar Square) and the Northern Line (at Strand) – as well as Charing Cross main line terminus.

The go-ahead was given in August 1971, with 75 per cent government financial support, and tunnelling began in February 1972. During the year of the Queen's Silver Jubilee in 1977 the GLC decided to rename the new line the Jubilee Line, which name it has been ever since. The Jubilee Line opened after considerable delay on 1st May 1979. On the same date the Bakerloo Line service reverted to its Watford Junction to Elephant & Castle routeing. Also, Charing Cross station was renamed Embankment, and Trafalgar Square (now part of an enlarged station serving the Jubilee Line) became Charing Cross.

The considerable work at Baker Street station during the Jubilee Line construction period caused a substantial deterioration in the platform finishings, which were still of BS&WR origin. A major renovation scheme was started which involved complete re-tiling of the Bakerloo Line platforms, escalator shafts, access passages and the intermediate concourse under the Metropolitan Line platforms. Following the theme begun on the Jubilee Line platforms, the new tiling was based on a repeating caricature of Sherlock Holmes's head, complete with pipe and deerstalker. The work was completed in 1982.

The loss of the Stanmore branch meant loss of ready access to the Bakerloo's main maintenance depot at Neasden, and an alternative was required. London Road depot had long since ceased to provide a major maintenance facility, and was now little more than a number of stabling sidings among ruined buildings. Initially it was hoped that extension to Peckham would offer opportunities for a major new depot, and a site between Peckham Rye and Nunhead was notionally set aside. When it became evident that the Peckham extension would not proceed and the depot would be needed close to the Elephant & Castle–Watford section, preferably close to the tube tunnel section which used the greater number of trains, the matter had become urgent.

The site eventually chosen was adjacent to the British Railways d.c. lines just north of Stonebridge Park station. Local residents were not pleased at the prospect of living next to a new depot (replacing the power station) and won several concessions at a planning inquiry on environmental grounds, but this did delay matters from the railway point of view. Preparatory re-signalling of the BR line in the Stonebridge Park area was commissioned in January 1977; the new depot itself was commissioned on 8th January 1979 and came into use from 9th April. Within the depot was an LT substation and a central control tower from where all train movements were controlled. There was a two-road lifting shop with six maintenance roads alongside, and seven other stabling sidings (six under cover).

Stonebridge Park depot also restored the Bakerloo Line's tie to the main line suburban tracks north of Queen's Park, an outlet which had seen little change in Underground service frequencies between the introduction of Sunday tube trains in 1919, and the mid 1960s, but which saw a drastic cut-back in through tube trains by the early 1970s. The latter history of this section of the Bakerloo Line is now looked at in more detail.

There had been few station alterations north of Queen's Park after 1919. A new station opened at South Kenton on 3rd July 1933 and Stonebridge Park (burnt down in 1917) was burnt down again in 1945 and rebuilt at platform level in 1948. Carpenders Park was relocated in 1952 (just south of the former station), though new buildings were not formally opened until 1954. New station buildings were also erected at Wembley Central and incorporated a shopping arcade; the work was started before the war, but completion was protracted.

The power supply arrangements north of Queen's Park carried on without much change until the 1940s when Stonebridge Park power station was updated and converted to 50-cycle operation with a capacity of 38 megawatts. New substation equipment was installed, largely at different locations than hitherto (between Watford and Queen's Park the locations were: Watford, Bushey, Hatch End, Harrow, Kenton, Wembley, Harlesden, Willesden and Queen's Park). The power station continued to operate until 30th July 1967 when current was obtained from the National Grid instead. The building survived a few years longer but was demolished prior to part of the site being used for the new Bakerloo Line depot.

The original Oerlikon stock used by British Railways on the Watford line had reached the end of its useful life by the mid 1950s and was replaced by new slam-door trains between 1957 and 1959 (one of the old Oerlikon cars is preserved in the National Railway Museum). The new stock was of unrevolutionary – even obsolescent – design, arranged in 3-car sets of mixed saloon and compartment formation, with one car on each set motored. In peak hours trains initially worked in 6-car formations. The BTH/GEC cars of 1928-32 vintage remained in service for a few more years, until service reductions meant they too could be scrapped.

However satisfactorily the Watford line may have served British Railways and its predecessors, the long haul out to Watford was never regarded as a great success by the Underground. Even prior to LPTB days the Watford service was considered to be rather unsatisfactory both in terms of its effect on reliability of the Bakerloo Line as a whole, and of the suitability of tube stock for passenger comfort on long distances and for relatively high-speed running.

Nevertheless the Bakerloo service remained at a fairly constant level until well after the Second World War; essentially a $7^{1}/_{2}$-minute peak interval between Queen's Park and Harrow, and 15 minutes northwards. Even as late as 1961 the LNWR scheme for separate services to three central London districts was still extant, with little change during the previous decade, though the pre-war preponderance of semi-fast main line electric trains had been much reduced.

SAMPLE D.C. LINE MORNING PEAK-HOUR SERVICE AT WILLESDEN JUNCTION IN 1961
(TRAINS FROM HIGH-LEVEL PLATFORMS EXCLUDED)

To	From	Trains	Total
Euston	Watford Junction	3	
	Croxley Green	1	4
Broad Street	Watford Junction	5	
(City)	Croxley Green	2	
	Bushey & Oxhey	1	8
Bakerloo Line	Watford Junction	5	
	Harrow & Wealdstone	3	8

GRAND TOTAL 20

During the midday off-peak period a basic 20-minute Bakerloo service operated to Watford Junction, with a Broad Street and a Euston service in between each of the Bakerloo trains. Not long after this date the local line services were progressively reduced as traffic levels dropped. One of the first casualties was the off-peak service from Watford to Broad Street, which ceased in August 1962.

A Bakerloo Line 1972 (Mk II) stock train joining the British Rail local lines just north of Stonebridge Park station. In the background may be seen the former LNWR maintenance sheds for the electric services. The new Underground depot, from where the train has come, is hidden behind. *Douglas Rose*

The reason for the previous stability of the tube service was not hard to see. As the track and the stations north of Queen's Park were owned by British Railways it was that organization which dictated service levels, and they paid LT to operate an appropriate number of trains. But it was the through off-peak Bakerloo Line service which was the next casualty of BR retrenchment. From the June 1965 timetable Bakerloo Line trains operated north of Queen's Park only in the rush hours, and through off-peak passengers had to change for the West End. Six Bakerloo trains ran south from Watford in the morning, and towards Watford in the evening, and an additional four trains ran to and from Harrow in both peaks. The BR services were also reduced further at the same time. The trains starting and finishing at Watford all stabled at Croxley Green shed.

The May 1966 timetable saw the through Watford trains reduced to four, one-way in each peak. The February 1970 timetable saw the four Harrow trains withdrawn (partly due to increasing unreliability of 1938 stock), leaving the Bakerloo Line with just four through Watford Junction trains in the rush hours, southbound in the morning and northbound in the evening. By this time the BR Watford service consisted of a 15-minute interval off-peak service between Watford Junction and Euston, with extra rush-hour trains to Broad Street about every 15 minutes. The maximum peak-hour service through Willesden Junction was now only 13 trains.

Also in 1970 the British Railways d.c. trains were converted from a 4-rail, insulated return, traction system to the 3-rail system widely used elsewhere on BR. To allow the Bakerloo Line trains to continue to operate north of Queen's Park the centre (fourth) rail was retained, but was bonded to one of the running rails and earthed (the negative rail was also retained south of Queen's Park to Kilburn High Road where there was an emergency crossover).

The 4-train Bakerloo service to Watford Junction was maintained for another decade, LT continuing to regard it as operationally convenient by using available train sidings at Croxley Green depot, while BR continued to pay for the trains which provided helpful peak capacity. From 1979, LT paid BR for trains running between Queen's Park and Stonebridge Park depot, BR regarding these as surplus to the basic Watford line timetable which itself had been reduced further during the mid 1970s. The 1974 London Rail Study had observed that the central London traffic from north of Queen's Park was split almost equally between BR and LT, though few LT passengers came from north of Harrow.

Until about 1977 train services throughout the Bakerloo Line continued to be provided by trains of 1938 stock (at this time peak services in the central area were at $1^1/2$–2-minute intervals). The pre-1938 stock trailers and the non-standard cars of 1949 origin had disappeared during the early 1970s when the fleet was rationalized, and the stock was latterly of standard formation. Many of the cars received a heavy overhaul from 1974 onwards, as it was considered that on the Bakerloo Line the stock would have a life extending into the 1980s. The obvious evidence of modification was the provision of 'outside door indicators', which illuminated if the doors on any car were open.

For the Fleet/Jubilee Line an interim order for new trains was made in 1972 in the form of 33 7-car trains known as the 1972 Mark II stock. These were initially put into service on the Northern Line to allow 1938 stock to be scrapped, but from 1977 they were gradually transferred to the Bakerloo Line where they operated alongside the 1938 stock, allowing staff to be trained and become familiar with the new trains. When the Jubilee Line opened in 1979 the 1972 stock was retained on the Stanmore (Jubilee) line service while the 1938 stock again became the mainstay of the Bakerloo. As a concession to Bakerloo Line staff who would otherwise have had to perform duty almost entirely in tunnel, both lines shared the same staff for some years after the Jubilee Line opening (about half the Jubilee Line mileage was in open air).

In 1982 the political and legal climate following the House of Lords judicial decision on LT subsidy caused widespread service reductions to meet more efficiently the prevailing passenger demand.

The reduced service level meant that the need to retain the LT stabling facilities at Croxley Green disappeared and the through service to Watford could no longer be justified. After several proposed withdrawal dates the last timetabled Bakerloo Line train actually departed from Watford Junction on the morning of 24th September 1982. From this date Bakerloo trains were not scheduled to work north of Stonebridge Park.

The loss of the service aroused adverse criticism and when the repercussions of the judicial decision had been finally settled, agreement was reached for a limited peak-hour service to be resumed as far as Harrow & Wealdstone, part of the costs being met by the Greater London Council. A 15-minute peak hour service to Harrow, running in both directions during each peak period, resumed from 4th June 1984. The Bakerloo Line service south of Stonebridge Park was roughly at 7 1/2-minute intervals.

The extended Bakerloo trains allowed British Rail to reduce the capacity of its own trains by introducing modern 3-car class 313 multiple units of 1976 construction (displaced from the Eastern Region) in lieu of the 1957-59 origin 6-car trains which were withdrawn or scrapped.

The 1938 tube stock began to deteriorate rapidly as it continued its fifth decade of service. Small builds of stock elsewhere on the Underground, together with general service reductions, allowed 1959 stock to be released from the Northern Line. The first 1959 stock train entered service on the Bakerloo on 28th February 1983 and the last train of 1938 stock was withdrawn on 20th November 1985. The 1959 stock was a stop-gap, as the desire to convert the Bakerloo Line to one-person train operation required more modern trains. Some 14 trains of 1959 stock were exchanged for a similar number of 1972 Mark II stock trains during summer 1986 (this was over 40 per cent of the Bakerloo's stockholding) to allow the technical work of conversion to begin.

Meanwhile a lull in the large-scale purchase of new Underground rolling stock allowed money to be diverted towards station refurbishments. Apart from Baker Street, Charing Cross was another station where the Jubilee Line had shown up the Bakerloo as old fashioned, and major refurbishment of the platforms was authorized in 1981. What emerged in 1983 was strikingly different to the appearance of the old platforms, and consisted of white melamine panels on which were printed colour pictures based on paintings in the nearby National Gallery. The whole scheme benefited from additional, concealed lighting. One of the more difficult jobs undertaken next was the refurbishment of the period ticket hall at Piccadilly Circus, restoring it to its 1920s splendour; the work was especially complicated in that the opportunity was taken to widen nearly all the access

Trafalgar Square station was renamed Charing Cross when the Jubilee Line opened in 1979, and the station became part of the complex also served by the Jubilee and Northern Lines. The platforms were still much as they had been when the station opened in 1906 but were soon modernized to suit the rest of the enlarged station, the work being completed in 1983. The decoration includes large coloured panels bearing images from the nearby National Gallery.

Douglas Rose

subways as part of the scheme. The work was completed in 1989.

By comparison with Charing Cross, platform refurbishments at Waterloo, Embankment, Piccadilly Circus, Oxford Circus and Paddington were comparatively mundane, though bringing new tile-work designs underground. Each had a different style. Paddington and Oxford Circus were thematic, the former incorporating a motif based on an early tunnelling machine and the latter based on a 'snakes & ladders' pattern.

The early 1970s had seen the beginning of a massive programme designed to update the Underground's lifts and escalators, and this continued throughout the 1980s. Except at Waterloo (Shell), Marylebone and those stations which became part of the Jubilee Line, many of the escalators on the Bakerloo Line had been of the 'L' type installed during the 1920s. In some cases over fifty years old, they were progressively withdrawn from service and totally refurbished, the resulting machines having much new running gear, with brushed steel panelling and metal treads instead of wooden components. At Embankment, Baker Street, Warwick Avenue, Maida Vale and Kilburn Park the original escalators of pre-1920 origin still existed, though these had been modernized and updated before the Second World War and the 'shunt' type landings replaced with the later standard type with cleated steps and combs. These machines were progressively replaced with modern machines once the L type escalators had been finished; the programme was completed by 1988.

The Bakerloo Line had retained the original Otis lifts at Elephant & Castle, Lambeth North, Waterloo, Regent's Park and Edgware Road until comparatively recent times. The lifts at Waterloo had been withdrawn from service in March 1973, following the introduction (in 1970) of two additional escalators and an enlarged ticket hall, adjacent to the existing shaft which came up beneath the main line station. At the remaining stations it was proposed to replace the existing lifts by new ones in the same shafts. At Regent's Park the decision was taken to withdraw the lift service completely from September 1984 while the existing lifts were replaced, the new ones coming into use in January 1987 (problems had arisen in replacing the lifts one at a time). Similarly, Lambeth North was without lifts while the old pair was replaced between June 1986 and February 1988. At both Elephant & Castle and Edgware Road the existing lifts occupied more than one shaft and it was possible to retain a lift service while replacement was under way.

Another project causing considerable changes to the public's perception was the huge amount of work undertaken from the end of 1986 to install the new systemwide Underground Ticketing System (UTS). The principal intention was to provide new high security ticket offices equipped with computerized ticket issuing equipment and passenger operated ticket machines which could be serviced from within the ticket office area. In central London, stations are equipped with automatic ticket gates to check all tickets on entry to and exit from the system. At outer stations it is proposed that existing (manual) ticket barriers eventually be removed, and tickets checked on a random basis with penalty fares charged if passengers are caught without a valid ticket.

A by-product of the new ticket system is that all the old-fashioned ticket offices were swept away. These included the free-standing booths known as Passimeters the first of which was introduced at Kilburn Park station in 1921. Under the Passimeter system the original idea was that the booking clerk at quiet times both issued tickets, checked tickets already held by inwards passengers, and checked or collected tickets of outwards passengers. This system became quite widespread in the 1920s and 1930s but largely fell into disuse after the war, although the booths remained for ticket issuing. Co-incidentally, the passimeter system remained substantially intact at Warwick Avenue, Maida Vale and Kilburn Park until UTS arrived.

In the early 1980s it became known that the government proposed to abolish the GLC, and as a preparatory measure restructured London Transport once more as a nationalized industry reporting to the Secretary of State for Transport. The new body, known as London Regional Transport, came into existence on Friday 29th June 1984, just three days after the London Regional Transport Act received the Royal Assent. Under a provision of that Act a subsidiary company was established on 29th March 1985 called London Underground Limited and on 1st April 1985 London Regional Transport's railway interests passed to this subsidiary company.

The upswing in London's economy, together with the introduction of fare zones and the Travelcard had started a boom in passenger travel, which still continues though now at a slower pace. Passenger journeys on the Underground have risen by over 50 per cent since 1981, and this has brought an urgent need for expanded service frequencies and additional trains. New stock deliveries and re-alloca-

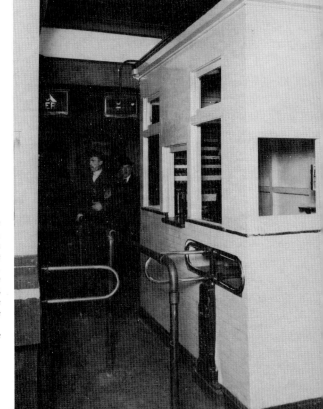

The first passimeter ticket office on the Underground was at Kilburn Park, which came into use on Friday 16th December 1921. Passimeters were later constructed in large numbers, often built of wood and to what one could be forgiven for thinking is a standard design. The office shown here was later replaced by one of more conventional pattern.

M.A.C. Horne collection

tions have allowed the remaining Bakerloo 1959 stock to be returned to the Northern Line in exchange for further 1972 Mark II stock, which, from early 1989, provides the whole of the Bakerloo Line service. Following the necessary technical work during 1988/9 trains are now equipped for one-person operation (trains began operation without guards in November 1989).

Government approval for joint LT/BR Capitalcards from January 1985 and the launch of 'Network SouthEast' in 1986 have helped substantially to revive passenger business on BR-owned lines in the London area. The growth in demand led to pressure for resumption of through weekday off-peak trains from Harrow & Wealdstone to the Bakerloo Line, after their 20-year absence. These were finally re-introduced from 16th May 1988 at 20-minute intervals (fulfilling a suggestion in the 1974 Rail Study). Travelcard availability was extended to Harrow & Wealdstone at the same time. From 15th May 1989 a Sunday Bakerloo Line service was introduced to Harrow, at 30-minute intervals. Not all the news was good – from 2nd October 1989 BR reduced the Watford via Primrose Hill to the City service to a single train a day (with three more from Willesden) each way.

In December 1988 the unique signalling system on the d.c. lines between Primrose Hill and Watford Junction was taken out of use and replaced with modern 2- or 3-aspect signals, power operated points and position-light shunt signals. Trackwork was largely unaltered but the emergency crossover at Kilburn High Road was moved to the north end of the platforms. Trainstops were provided on sections between Kilburn High Road and Harrow, over which section Bakerloo Line trains operate. Earlier in the year one of the twin sidings at Harrow was removed (there had been two sidings here since 1932) and a new crossover was provided south of the station.

Work has also begun on resignalling the Bakerloo Line and the construction of a new signalling control centre at Baker Street, to replace the existing signal cabins. Most of the signalling between Queen's Park and Baker Street has been replaced, and work continues.

With traffic levels soaring, relatively modern trains, new signalling and many refurbished stations, the future of the line is bright. Possible extension schemes are being considered for the 'in-town' section of the line south of Queen's Park, while to the north the line's future depends equally as much on British Rail decisions on new investment and on service levels, but traffic is buoyant. It will have become clear to the reader that the inextricable link with the British Rail operation north of Queen's Park makes the Bakerloo Line a more complex animal than its straightforward portrayal on the Underground diagram might have implied.